Comfort

Quotations
From the
Writings of
Ellen G. White

Pacific Press Publishing Association
Boise, Idaho
Oshawa, Ontario, Canada

Cover Photo By Robert Holmes/The Corbis Collections

Copyright 1996
Pacific Press Publishg Association
Printed in United States of America
All Rights Reserved

ISBN 0-8163-1367-9

96 97 98 99 00 • 5 4 3 2 1

We all experience times when we are in need of comfort—the death of a loved one, or loss of a cherished dream; disappointment with others or ourselves; the loss of employment; discovery of illness; times of pain. These are the experiences that try our souls and test our faith.

None of us is strong enough to bear up under life's great disappointments and trials alone. We all need the help of one another, and especially the help of Him who promised to send us "another comforter" (John 14:16).

This little book draws upon the experience and writings of one who knew Jesus as a personal friend—a Friend whom she spoke with often, and who often gave special messages to her. Ellen White also knew times of great trial. Some might think that her sense of God's leading would spare her from doubt and the temptation to wonder whether heaven's plan was truly being fulfilled in her life, but she was just as subject to such questions as any of us.

Out of these experiences of trial came a great compassion and urgency to help others who were beset by temptation. Many of her letters were written to people who were struggling through temptation and doubt that resulted from trial.

Here, drawn from the vast resource of her preserved writings, are some of the most comforting passages that she penned to others who needed comfort, and to all of us who need to understand how to find comfort in Jesus.

We hope that many will find comfort and encouragement by turning to these short quotations in times of need, and simply at times when a comforting word will give the added boost they need to make it through the day.

—The Compilers

*W*hen our hopes of life seem to be slipping away,
Jesus is ready to put his everlasting arms beneath us,
and to draw us to his heart,
and to comfort, encourage, and bless us.

ST 17 March 1890

$\mathcal{T}$hose who have humbly sought God
for comfort and peace in the midst of trial,
have had imparted to them the gentleness of Christ.

ST 22 August 1895

$\mathcal{L}$et every mourner look up and be comforted.
Every service rendered to the Master in helping others,
is blessing yourself, and the benediction that is spoken
to those that mourn,
will result in your own comforting.

ST 15 August 1898

In a world of sin
Jesus endured struggles and torture of soul.
In communion with God
He could unburden the sorrows that were crushing Him.
Here He found comfort and joy.

DA 362

The power of the truth should be sufficient
to sustain and console in every adversity.
It is in enabling its possessor
to triumph over affliction
that the religion of Christ reveals its true value.

1MCP 235

The power of speech is a sacred trust to be improved
to exalt the plan of redemption and magnify its Author,
to speak words of comfort
to the discouraged and desponding,
to speak kind and pleasant words
that shall be as a refreshing draught
to those who are thirsting for sympathy and love.

ST 20 November 1884

Christ himself trod a more thorny path
than any of his followers.
They may comfort themselves with the thought
that they are in good company.

ST 21 June 1883

The path may be steep and rugged,
but Jesus has traveled that way;
His feet have pressed down the cruel thorns,
to make the pathway easier for us.
Every burden that we are called to bear
He Himself has borne.

DA 480

$\mathcal{L}$et us study the words that Christ spoke
in the upper chamber on the night before His crucifixion.
He was nearing His hour of trial,
and He sought to comfort His disciples,
who were to be so severely tempted and tried.

MH 419

God does not prevent the plottings of wicked men,
but He causes their devices to work for good
to those who in trial and conflict
maintain their faith and loyalty.

RY 177

$\mathcal{L}$et us look at the light behind the cloud.
O, how much of comfort
the murmurers and complainers lose
in not bearing all things patiently!

RH 27 February 1894

*W*herever there were hearts
ready to receive His message,
He comforted them with the assurance
of their heavenly Father's love.

GW 42

As trouble in the world increases,
the Lord's children will have to suffer;
but the Word of God affords
comfort and encouragement for such a time.
Read the first and second chapters of First Corinthians;
there are precious assurances here for the child of God.

RH 29 July 1909

*O*ften He met those
who had drifted under Satan's control,
and who had no power to break from his snare.
To such a one, discouraged, sick, tempted, fallen,
Jesus would speak words of tenderest pity. . . .

MH 26

*T*hen talk of the promises;
talk of Jesus' willingness to bless.
He does not forget us for one brief moment.
When, notwithstanding disagreeable circumstances,
we rest confidingly in His love,
and shut ourselves in with Him,
the sense of His presence will inspire a deep, tranquil joy.

MH 488

The word of God is to be our daily teacher.
This is the only true source of comfort in all our trials,
the only true source of encouragement
and instruction in our labors.

TDG 281

These words from the lips of the Saviour,
traced by the inspired John in chapters
fifteen, sixteen, and seventeen,
were repeated again and again
by the disciples to stay their sinking hearts
in their great disappointment and trial.

3SP 88, 89

And the promise of Christ's presence
in answer to prayer should comfort and encourage
his church to-day as much as it comforted and encouraged
the apostles whom Christ directly addressed.

3SP 247

In the word of God there are gracious promises,
from which those who are suffering,
whether in body or in mind,
may receive comfort and hope and encouragement.

CH 213

Our happiness comes not from what is around us,
but from what is within us;
not from what we have,
but from what we are.

ML 185

A consecrated Christian life
is ever shedding light and comfort and peace.

AG 122

The Lord has special grace for the mourner,
and its power is to melt hearts, to win souls.
His love opens a channel
into the wounded and bruised soul,
and becomes a healing balsam to those who sorrow.

AG 122

From every temptation and every trial
[Christ] will bring them forth
with firmer faith and a richer experience.

DA 528

It is your privilege to receive grace from Christ
that will enable you to comfort others
with the same comfort wherewith you yourselves
are comforted of God.

AG 122

All over the field of revelation
are scattered grains of gold. . . .
If you are wise
you will gather up these precious grains of truth.
Make the promises of God your own.
Then when test and trial come,
these promises will be to you
glad springs of heavenly comfort.

TMK 202

Christ found comfort and joy
in communion with His Father.
Here He could unburden His heart
of the sorrows that were crushing Him.
He was a man of sorrows and acquainted with grief.

2T 202

To all who are reaching out
to feel the guiding hand of God,
the moment of greatest discouragement
is the time when divine help is nearest.
They will look back with thankfulness
upon the darkest part of their way.

DA 528

*O*h, how thankful my soul is in your behalf,
that in your bereavement and trial
that the One who was a man of sorrows
and acquainted with grief . . .
can take in all your wants, your trials,
your suffering, your loneliness.
The Lord Jesus is your helper, your restorer.

TSA 76

2—COMFORT

The trials that come to the members of His church
are sent for their purification and their advancement.
In times of darkness, let us not despond.
Let us comfort our hearts by remembering
that if we walk and work with God,
in humility and sincerity,
He will be our joy and peace and hope,
and will give us precious victories.

AUCR 15 June 1902

The Lord Jesus is your helper, your restorer.
The Giver of all blessings will comfort and bless
and strengthen you and all who suffer
in doing His work.

TSA 76

*T*hose who have borne the greatest sorrows
are frequently the ones who carry the greatest comfort
to others, bringing sunshine wherever they go.

AG 122

Every soul is as fully known to Jesus
as if he were the only one for whom the Saviour died.
The distress of every one touches His heart.
The cry for aid reaches His ear.

DA 480

*H*is heart was pierced with the pain
of the human family of all ages and in all lands.
The woes of the sinful race were heavy upon His soul,
and the fountain of His tears was broken up
as He longed to relieve all their distress.

DA 534

We miss very much
because we do not grasp the blessings
that may be ours in our afflictions.
All our sufferings and sorrows,
all our temptations and trials,
all our sadness and griefs,
all our persecutions and privations,
and in short all things, work together for our good.

ML 185

We are to find our consolation in Jesus Christ.
Precious Saviour!
He was ever touched with human woe. . . .
Cling to the Source of your strength.

2SM 264

For a little season they might be in heaviness . . .
they might be destitute of earthly comfort;
but they could encourage their hearts
with the assurance of God's faithfulness, saying,
"I know whom I have believed,
and am persuaded that He is able to keep
that which I have committed unto Him."

2MCP 463

The faith that will bring us peace
in sorrow and tribulation is the faith we must all have,
for it is an anchor to the soul,
entering into that within the veil.

ST 08 June 1891

Christ represents death as a sleep
to His believing children.
Their life is hid with Christ in God,
and until the last trump shall sound
those who die will sleep in Him.

DA 527

Those who surrender their lives to His guidance and to His service will never be placed in a position for which He has not made provision.

MH 248

In times of sorrow or joy
we all need a Saviour to love us,
and he is at our right hand
to help and comfort
in every time of trial and affliction.

ST 8 June 1891

*T*hrough the Holy Spirit,
that voice which was speaking from the fisherman's boat
on the Sea of Galilee,
would be heard speaking peace to human hearts
to the close of time.

DA 245

Christ's servants are to follow His example.
As He went from place to place,
He comforted the suffering and healed the sick.
Then He placed before them the great truths
in regard to His kingdom.

COL 233

The trial of faith is more precious than gold.
All should learn that this is a part of the discipline
in the school of Christ,
which is essential to purify and refine them
from the dross of earthliness.

AG 73

*T*he plans of the enemies of His work
may seem to be . . . firmly established,
but God can overthrow the strongest of these.
And this He does . . . when He sees that the faith
of His servants has been sufficiently tested.

PK 164

O, it is not weakness to have a tender,
humble, sympathetic, pitying heart.
Of this no one should be ashamed
as if it were a weakness.
It is strength derived from Christ.

1888 Materials 1466

The trials of one may not be the trials of another;
and our hearts should ever be open to kindly sympathy,
and aglow with the divine love
that Jesus manifested for all his brethren.

ST 3 March 1887

Make the promises of God your own.
Then when test and trial come,
these promises will be to you
glad springs of heavenly comfort.

ML 28

The mission of Christ to this world
was to heal the broken-hearted.
He received mourners,
and comforted those who were sorrow-stricken,
those who had lost courage and hope.
Upon such he pronounced his blessing,
and declared they should be comforted.

ST 8 August 1895

Our sorrows do not spring out of the ground.
God "doth not afflict willingly
nor grieve the children of men."
When He permits trials and afflictions,
it is "for our profit,
that we might be partakers of His holiness."

SD 302

*T*hose who look within for comfort
will become weary and disappointed.
A sense of our weakness and unworthiness
should lead us with humility of heart
to plead the atoning sacrifice of Christ.

5T 200

*L*et us look to the monumental pillars,
reminders of what the Lord has done to comfort us
and to save us from the hand of the destroyer.
Let us keep fresh in our memory all the tender mercies
that God has shown us,—the tears He has wiped away,
the pains He has soothed, the anxieties removed,
the fears dispelled, the wants supplied,
the blessings bestowed,—
thus strengthening ourselves for all that is before us
through the remainder of our pilgrimage.

SC 125

If received in faith,
the trial that seems so bitter and hard to bear
will prove a blessing. . . .
How many there are who would never have known Jesus
had not sorrow led them to seek comfort in Him!

SD 302

Christ has been manifested to the world
as the One who can bind up the broken in heart,
and comfort those that mourn.
Heaven was open to man
through the sacrifice of the Son of God.

ST 29 July 1889

In the religious life of every soul
who is finally victorious
there will be scenes of terrible perplexity and trial;
but his knowledge of the Scriptures
will enable him to bring to mind
the encouraging promises of God. . . .

AG 73

*T*here is joy and satisfaction in the service of God;
the Christian is not left to walk in uncertain paths;
he is not left to vain regrets and disappointments.
If we do not have the pleasures of this life
we may still be joyful in looking to the life beyond.

SC 124, 125

If it does not sustain you in trial
and comfort you in affliction,
it is because your faith has not been made strong
by effort and pure by sacrifice.

2SM 166

This life will be much brighter for us
if we will gather the flowers and leave the briers alone.
Comfort, encouragement, and support
have been provided for every circumstance
and condition of life.

ST 27 July 1904

Christ himself will brighten your gloom
with bright gleams of light,
and his divine light will be all the more precious
and glorious as it shines forth amid clouds and darkness.
"Blessed are they that mourn;
for they shall be comforted."

ST 15 August 1898

Oh, how good it would be to meet
with a few of like precious faith
to exhort and comfort one another
with words of holy cheer from the word of God.
The sheep are now scattered,
but thank God they are about to be gathered
to a good pasture.

5MR 95

We have reason to be comforted.
Severe outward trials may press around
the soul where Jesus lives.
Let us turn to Him for the consolations
He has provided for us in His Word.

TDG 62

The experience to be gained
in the furnace of trial and affliction is worth more
than all the pain it costs.
Thus God brings His children near to Him,
that He may show them their weakness and His strength.
He teaches them to lean on Him.

RY 176, 177

The path of holiness is narrow,
full of self-denial and continual sacrifice;
and yet in this laborious, up-hill path
is happiness, comfort, and hope.
In the midst of conflicts, rebuffs, and trials,
the most elevated consolation
is enjoyed by those who walk in the path of obedience.

RH 15 April 1880

Those who have learned of Him
who is meek and lowly of heart,
express sympathy, and manifest gentleness
toward those who are in need of consolation;
for they can comfort others with the consolation
wherewith they are comforted of God.

ST 22 August 1895

Apparently Mary and Martha
and the dying Lazarus were left alone.
But they were not alone.
Christ beheld the whole scene,
and after the death of Lazarus
the bereaved sisters were upheld by His grace.

DA 528

How full of comfort and love
are the words of Christ to his disciples
just before his trial and crucifixion.
He was about to leave them,
but he did not want them to think
that they were to be left helpless orphans.

RH 27 January 1903

You need not pour your troubles into human ears;
for it will do you little good. You may think it will help you,
but there is only One who can give you
comfort and strength.
Jesus has said, "Come unto me,
all ye that labor and are heavy laden,
and I will give you rest."

RH 28 January 1890

In every trial, if we seek Him,
Christ will give us help.
Our eyes will be opened
to discern the healing promises recorded in His word.
The Holy Spirit will teach us how to appropriate
every blessing that will be an antidote to grief.
For every bitter draft that is placed to our lips,
we shall find a branch of healing.

MH 248

If in our ignorance we make missteps,
the Saviour does not forsake us.
We need never feel that we are alone.
Angels are our companions.
The Comforter that Christ promised to send in His name
abides with us.

MH 249

If the Lord bows His ear to hear your cry,
to relieve you in trial, to comfort you in bereavement,
to bind up your wounds,
to sustain you in all your heart-trying tribulations,
you know it is because he loves you.

HM 1 July 1891

*B*y the grace of Christ,
we may be composed
and even cheerful under sore trial.

RY 160

*T*he Lord would have every one come to him
as their Refuge, for counsel, and for comfort, and for hope,
in all their anxieties. To him you may tell all your griefs.
You will never be told, "I cannot help you."

ST 7 October 1897

When trials and tribulations come to you
know that they are sent in order
that you may receive from the Lord of glory
renewed strength and increased humility. . . .
In faith and with the hope that "maketh not ashamed,"
lay hold of the promises of God.

ML 185

The afflicted ones who came to Him
felt that He linked His interest with theirs
as a faithful and tender friend,
and they desired to know more of the truths He taught.

DA 254, 255

Your Father was by your side,
bending over you with unutterable love,
afflicting you for your good,
as the refiner purifies the precious ore.

GW (1892 ed.) 373

For the disheartened there is a sure remedy—
faith, prayer, work.
Faith and activity will impart assurance and satisfaction
that will increase day by day.

PK 164

As you review the past with a clear vision,
you will see that at the very time
when life seemed to you only a perplexity and a burden,
Jesus himself was near you,
seeking to lead you into the light.

GW (1892 ed.) 373

Temptations and trials may come,
but that is not an evidence that you are not a child of God.
He wants you to pray.
Take hold of him for strength and comfort.

GCB 23 April 1901

*W*hen we are in trial, when we are opposed
and in difficulty, when reports are made in regard to us . . .
we should stand where we shall not retaliate,
but reveal Christ.

GCB 23 April 1901

God's love for His children
during the period of their severest trial
is as strong and tender
as in the days of their sunniest prosperity. . . .

GC 621

It was the compassionate Saviour, who,
anticipating the loneliness and sorrow of His followers,
commissioned angels to comfort them
with the assurance that He would come again in person,
even as He went into heaven.

GC 339

*A*re you tempted to give way
to feelings of anxious foreboding or utter despondency?
In the darkest days, when appearances
seem most forbidding, fear not.
Have faith in God. He knows your need.
He has all power.

PK 164

I am sorry, my sister,
that you are in affliction and sorrow.
But Jesus, the precious Saviour, lives.
He lives for you.
He wants you to be comforted in His love.

RY 159

Our heavenly Father has a thousand ways
to provide for us of which we know nothing.
Those who accept the one principle of
making the service of God supreme,
will find perplexities vanish
and a plain path before their feet.

MH 481

$\mathcal{K}$eep the heart full of the precious promises of God,
that you may bring forth from this treasure,
words that will be a comfort and strength to others.

MH 257

Jesus comforts our sorrow for the dead
with a message of infinite hope:
"I am He that liveth, and was dead;
and, behold, I am alive forevermore, . . .
and have the keys of hell and of death" (Rev. 1:18).

DA 32

*W*ith the deepest interest
Jesus poured forth the burden of his soul
in words of comfort, of counsel and prayer,
which would ever remain imprinted
on the minds and hearts of his disciples.

3SP 88 , 89

*W*hen you have thought yourself forsaken,
He has been near you to comfort and sustain.
We seldom view Jesus as He is,
and are never so ready to receive His help
as He is to help us.

4T 221

Though He was the Son of God,
yet He had taken human nature upon Him,
and He was moved by human sorrow.
His tender, pitying heart is ever awakened
to sympathy by suffering.
He weeps with those that weep,
and rejoices with those that rejoice.

DA 533

He sought to inspire with hope
the roughest and most unpromising,
setting before them the assurance
that they might become blameless and harmless,
attaining such a character as would make them
manifest as the children of God.

MH 25

*T*hose who suffer most
have most of His sympathy and pity.
He is touched with the feeling of our infirmities,
and He desires us to lay our perplexities and troubles
at His feet and leave them there.

MH 249

In nature itself are messages of hope and comfort.
There are flowers upon the thistles,
and the thorns are covered with roses.

SC 10

The very trials that test our faith most severely,
and make it seem that God has forsaken us,
are designed to lead us nearer to Christ,
that we may lay all our burdens at his feet,
and receive the peace he will give us in exchange.

GW (1892 ed.) 372

Christ is our example, not only in His spotless purity,
but in His patience, gentleness,
and winsomeness of disposition.
His life is an illustration of true courtesy.
He had ever a kind look and a word of comfort
for the needy and the oppressed.
His presence brought a purer atmosphere into the home.

CM 73

*W*hat a busy life He led!
Day by day He might have been seen
entering the humble abodes of want and sorrow,
speaking hope to the downcast
and peace to the distressed.

MH 24

He comforted the weak,
the trembling, and the desponding.
The feeble, suffering ones whom Satan held in triumph,
Jesus wrenched from his grasp,
bringing to them soundness of body
and great joy and happiness.

EW 159

For every trial,
God has provided help.

MH 248

Gracious, tenderhearted, pitiful,
He went about lifting up the bowed-down
and comforting the sorrowful.
Wherever He went, He carried blessing.

MH 24

All experiences and circumstances
are God's workmen whereby good is brought to us.
Let us look at the light behind the cloud.

ML 185

Not only does Christ know every soul,
and the peculiar needs and trials of that soul,
but He knows all the circumstances
that chafe and perplex the spirit.
His hand is outstretched in pitying tenderness
to every suffering child.

MH 249

*N*one need abandon themselves
to discouragement and despair.
Satan may come to you with the cruel suggestion,
"Yours is a hopeless case. You are irredeemable."
But there is hope for you in Christ.

MH 249

On the way that leads to the City of God
there are no difficulties which those who trust in Him
may not overcome.
There are no dangers which they may not escape.
There is not a sorrow, not a grievance,
not a human weakness,
for which He has not provided a remedy.

MH 249

*W*hile the Lord has not promised
His people exemption from trials,
He has promised that which is far better.
He has said, "As thy days, so shall thy strength be"
(Deuteronomy 33:25).

MB 30

There is in spiritual lines of work
that which keeps the spirits cheered,
uplifted, and comforted.

Ev 468

He healed the sick, comforted the mourning,
called the dead to life, and brought hope
and cheer to the despairing.
After His work for the day was finished,
He went forth, evening after evening,
away from the confusion of the city,
and bowed in prayer to His Father.

GW 256

There is comfort and joy in the service of Christ.
Let the world see that life with Him is no failure.

GW 477

We need not keep our own record
of trials and difficulties, griefs, and sorrows.
All these things are written in the books,
and heaven will take care of them.

GW 477

We will look to the monumental pillars,
reminders of what the Lord has done,
to comfort us and to save us
from the hand of the destroyer.
We want to have fresh in our memory
every tear the Lord has wiped from our eyes. . .

GW (1892 ed.) 374

It is the work of faith
to rest in God in the darkest hour,
to feel, however sorely tried and tempest tossed,
that our Father is at the helm.
The eye of faith alone can look beyond
the things of time to estimate aright
the worth of eternal riches.

RY 178

If you are called to go through
the fiery furnace for His sake,
Jesus will be by your side
even as He was with the faithful three in Babylon.

MB 30

What benevolence, what compassion,
what tender sympathy, Jesus has manifested
toward suffering humanity!
The heart that beats in unison
with His great heart of infinite love
will give sympathy to every needy soul,
and will make it manifest
that he has the mind of Christ.

LHU 206

The Saviour knows our inmost thought,
and cannot judge our actions wrongly.
We may tell him all our griefs and perplexities,
and he will never abuse our confidence,
nor turn a deaf ear to our complaints.

HR 1 October 1877

*L*et the thought encourage us
that Christ pities the erring,
and desires to comfort the despondent,
and encourage the weak.
He is fully acquainted with the peculiar trials of every life.
He never misjudges our motives,
nor places a wrong estimate upon our character.

HR 1 October 1877

A single ray of the evidences
of the undeserved favor of God
shining into our hearts
will overbalance every trial
of whatever character
and however severe it may be.

OHC 323

Whatever your anxieties and trials,
spread out your case before the Lord.
Your spirit will be braced for endurance.

MH 72

*H*uman love may change,
but Christ's love knows no change.
When we cry to Him for help,
His hand is stretched out to save.

MH 72

At all times and in all places,
in all sorrows and in all afflictions,
when the outlook seems dark and the future perplexing,
and we feel helpless and alone,
the Comforter will be sent
in answer to the prayer of faith.

FLB 56

Circumstances may separate us from every earthly friend;
but no circumstance, no distance,
can separate us from the heavenly Comforter.
Wherever we are, wherever we may go,
He is always at our right hand
to support, sustain, uphold, and cheer.

FLB 56

The weaker and more helpless you know yourself to be,
the stronger will you become in His strength.
The heavier your burdens, the more blessed the rest
in casting them upon your Burden Bearer.

MH 72

God will not suffer one of His truehearted workers
to be left alone,
to struggle against great odds and be overcome.
He preserves as a precious jewel
everyone whose life is hid with Christ in Him.

MH 488

Whatever our situation, if we are doers of His word,
we have a Guide to direct our way;
whatever our perplexity, we have a sure Counselor;
whatever our sorrow, bereavement, or loneliness,
we have a sympathizing Friend.

MH 248, 249

$\mathcal{J}$esus stands by our side. . . .
As the trials come,
the power of God will come with them.

ML 184

Do not go about as if Jesus were in Joseph's tomb,
and a great stone were rolled before the door. . . .
In the trial of your faith
show that you know you have a risen Saviour,
One who is making intercession
for you and your loved ones.

ML 184

*W*herever we may be, He is at our right hand,
to support, maintain, uphold, and cheer.
Greater than the love of a mother for her child
is Christ's love for His redeemed.

MH 72

When all seems dark and unexplainable
we are to trust in His love;
we must repeat the words
that Christ has spoken to our souls,
"What I do thou knowest not now;
but thou shalt know hereafter."

ML 184

*O*ften our trials are such
that they seem almost unbearable,
and without help from God
they are indeed unbearable. . . .
But if we make Christ our dependence,
we shall not sink under trial.

ML 184

If you are looking to Jesus
and drawing from Him knowledge and strength and grace,
you can impart His consolation to others,
because the Comforter is with you.

CH 34

Circumstances may separate friends;
the restless waters of the wide sea
may roll between us and them.
But no circumstances, no distance,
can separate us from the Saviour.

MH 72

By comforting others,
they themselves will be comforted.

ChS 151

Come close to the great heart of pitying love,
and let the current of that divine compassion
flow into your heart and from you
to the hearts of others.

AG 226

Peter realized that in the experience of every soul
who is finally victorious
there would be scenes of perplexity and trial;
but he knew also that an understanding of the Scriptures
would enable the tempted one to bring to mind
promises that would comfort the heart
and strengthen faith in the Mighty One.

AA 521

The trial will not exceed the strength
that shall be given us to bear it.
Then let us take up our work just where we find it,
believing that whatever may come,
strength proportionate to the trial will be given.

SC 125

Find time to comfort some other heart,
to bless with a kind, cheering word. . . .
In thus blessing another . . .
you may unexpectedly find peace, happiness,
and consolation yourself.

AG 122

Our heavenly Father measures and weighs every trial
before He permits it to come upon the believer.
He considers the circumstances and the strength
of the one who is to stand
under the proving and test of God,
and He never permits the temptations
to be greater than the capacity of resistance.

OHC 323

Trust Him with all your heart.
He will carry you and your burdens.

ML 185

KEY TO ABBREVIATED TITLES

1888 Materials	*The Ellen G. White 1888 Materials*
1MCP, 2MCP	*Mind Character and Personality* (2 vols.)
2SM	*Selected Messages,* book 2
2T, 4T, etc.	*Testimonies for the Church,* (9 vols.)
3SP	*The Spirit of Prophecy,* vol. 3
5MR	*Manuscript Releases,* vol. 5
AA	*Acts of the Apostles*
AG	*God's Amazing Grace*
AUCR	*Australian Union Conference Record*
CH	*Counsels on Health*
ChS	*Christian Service*
CM	*Colporteur Ministry*

COL	*Christ's Object Lessons*
DA	*Desire of Ages*
Ev	*Evangelism*
EW	*Early Writings*
FLB	*The Faith I Live By*
GC	*The Great Controversy*
GCB	*General Conference Bulletin*
GW	*Gospel Workers*
HM	*The Home Missionary*
HR	*The Health Reformer*
LHU	*Lift Him Up*
MB	*Thoughts From the Mount of Blessing*
MH	*The Ministry of Healing*
ML	*My Life Today*

OHC	*Our High Calling*
PK	*Patriarchs and Prophets*
RH	*The Adventist Review and Sabbath Herald*
RY	*Retirement Years*
SC	*Steps to Christ*
SD	*Sons and Daughters of God*
ST	*Signs of the Times*
TDG	*This Day With God*
TMK	*That I May Know Him*
TSA	*Testimonies to Southern Africa*